Álvaro Leite Siza Vieira | Porto, Portugal
Casa Tóló
Alvite, Portugal | 2005

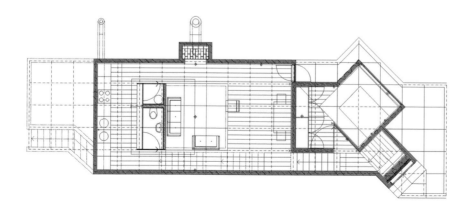

Das Feuer begleitet den Menschen schon seit den Anfängen der Zivilisation. Bis zur Entstehung moderner Heizungssysteme existierten in den meisten Häusern und Wohnungen in jeglicher Gesellschaftsschicht Öfen und Kamine. Dies konnten einfache Feuerstellen in den Küchen der unteren Gesellschaftsschichten sein, oder wundervolle Kamine in den Palästen. Der Kamin ist ein Element, das von Architekten und Industriedesignern ständig verändert und weiterentwickelt wurde. So gelang es mit der Zeit auch, die erzeugte Energie und Wärme zu optimieren und lästigen Rauch und Gerüche zu vermeiden. Der gemeinsame Zweck von Kaminen und Öfen nicht mehr einfach nur, eine Wohnung zu beheizen, sondern sie schaffen eine warme Atmosphäre, in der das Spiel der Flammen die Blicke wie ein Magnet auf sich zieht. Auf den folgenden Seiten zeigen wir Ihnen interessant gestaltete Kamine und Holz- oder Gasöfen aus verschiedenen Materialien.

Fire has accompanied man since the dawn of civilization. Until the appearance of modern heating systems, chimneys have been present in most homes, regardless of social status. From humble kitchen fireplaces, to the magnificent chimneys of palaces, this feature has developed at the hands of architects and industrial designers. Over the course of time designers have managed to optimise the heat and energy generated, and to avoid problems such as smoke and smells. However, heating the home is no longer the sole aim of chimneys and heaters. They create cosy, warm atmospheres, allowing us to enjoy the magnetism of their flames. The following pages present designs of both wood and gas fuelled chimneys and heaters, made from a variety of materials and original designs.

El fuego ha acompañado al hombre desde los albores de la civilización. Hasta la aparición de los modernos sistemas de climatización, las chimeneas han estado presentes en la mayoría de las viviendas de cualquier estrato social. Desde los humildes hogares de las cocinas hasta las magníficas chimeneas de los palacios, este elemento ha evolucionado de la mano de la arquitectura y del diseño industrial. Con el tiempo, se ha conseguido optimizar la energía y el calor que genera y evitar molestias como el humo y los olores. Asimismo, las chimeneas y estufas ya no tienen como único objetivo calentar el interior de la vivienda, sino que permiten crear atmósferas cálidas y disfrutar del magnetismo de las llamas. En las siguientes páginas se muestran algunos ejemplos de chimeneas y estufas de leña y gas, construidas con diversos materiales y a partir de diseños muy originales.

Le feu a accompagné l'Homme depuis l'aube de la civilisation. Jusqu'à l'apparition des systèmes modernes de climatisation, les cheminées étaient présentes dans la plupart des demeures, quel que soit le statut social des occupants. Des foyers les plus humbles des cuisines jusqu'aux magnifiques cheminées des palais, cet élément a évolué au rythme de l'architecture et du design industriel. Avec le temps, il est devenu possible d'optimiser l'énergie et la chaleur générées et d'éviter les gênes comme la fumée et les odeurs. De la sorte, les cheminées et les poêles n'ont plus seulement comme objectif de chauffer l'intérieur de la demeure mais bien de créer des atmosphères chaleureuses et de jouir du magnétisme des flammes. Les pages suivantes proposent des concepts de cheminées et de poêles au bois et au gaz, construits avec divers matériaux et à partir de design très originaux.

Il fuoco ha accompagnato l'uomo sin dagli albori della civiltà. Fino alla comparsa dei moderni sistemi di climatizzazione, i camini sono stati presenti nella maggior parte delle abitazioni di qualsiasi strato sociale. Dagli umili focolari delle cucine fino ai magnifici camini dei palazzi, questo elemento si è evoluto di pari passo con l'architettura e il design industriale. Con passar del tempo, si è riusciti ad ottimizzare l'energia e il calore che genera ed evitare inconvenienti quali il fumo e gli odori. Comunque, i camini e le stufe non hanno più come unico obiettivo riscaldare l'interno di una abitazione, ma permettono inoltre di creare un'atmosfera calda e accogliente e di godere del magnetismo delle fiamme. Nelle pagine che seguono si mostrano alcuni esempi di camini e stufe, sia a legna che a gas, costruiti con diversi materiali e a partire da disegni molto originali.

new fireplace design

daab

Amorphe Takeyama & Associates/Kiyoshi Sey Takeyama
Kassai House
Osaka, Japan | 2003

Carlos Castanheira | Vila Nova de Gaia, Portugal
Casa C. Cast.
Gondomar, Portugal | 2005

CASA Akira Sakamoto Architect & Associates | Osaka, Japan
House in Habikigaoka
Osaka, Japan | 2004

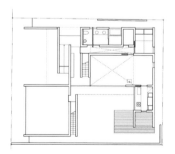
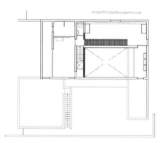
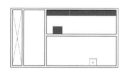

Claesson Koivisto Rune | Stockholm, Sweden
House Nº 5
Nacka, Sweden | 2003

Co. Twee | Antwerpen, Belgium
Flat in Schelde
Schelde, Belgium | 2001

Co. Twee | Antwerpen, Belgium
House in Knokke
Lommergang, Belgium | 2003

Costa Group | La Spezia, Italy
Hotel Sant Roc
Solsona, Lleida, Spain | 2004

D'Arcy Jones Design | Vancouver, Canada
Mosewich House
Kamloops, British Columbia, Canada | 2004

Delices Architectes/Jean Leclercq | Brussels, Belgium
Loft Louise
Brussels, Belgium | 2002

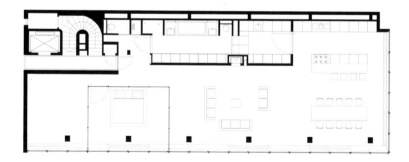

Dominique Imbert
Cromifocus | 2005
Focus

Dominique Imbert
Neofocus a bois, Renzofocus, Miofocus | 2005
Focus

EcoSmart Fire / Stephane Thomas
Oxygen | 2003
EcoSmart Fire

EDENA/Borgers Dumoulin | Brussels, Belgium
Interior design: Anne Derasse
Loft Wery XL
Brussels, Belgium | 2002

Frédéric Méchiche | Paris, France
Hotel Le A
Paris, France | 2004

Guido Micchiardi | Brussels, Belgium
Apartment in Temse
Temse, Belgium | 2001

Iván Hernández Esterlingot | Barcelona, Spain
House in Blanes
Blanes, Girona, Spain | 1999

Jaime Sanahuja y Asociados | Castellón, Spain
Villa +
Oropesa del Mar, Castellón, Spain | 2003

James Slade | New York, NY, USA
Loft Will Smith
New York, NY, USA | 2002

Joan Bach | Barcelona, Spain
House in Vallromanes
Vallromanes, Barcelona, Spain | 2001

John Pawson | London, UK
Telluride House
Telluride, CO, USA | 2001

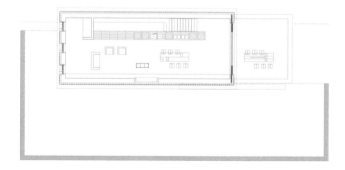

Jordi Galí Estudio | Barcelona, Spain
Apartment JG
Barcelona, Spain | 2002

Ken Yokogawa Architect & Associates | Yokohama, Japan
House in Tateshima
Tateshima, Japan | 2004

Laura Cavalca | Brescia, Italy
House in Brescia
Brescia, Italy | 1999

Lens Ass Architectuurbureau | Hasselt, Belgium
Donum
Hasselt, Belgium | 2000

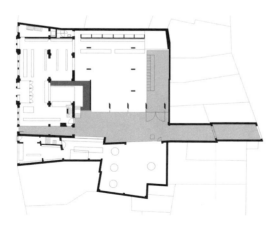

Lens Ass Architectuurbureau | Hasselt, Belgium
Loft in Hasselt
Hasselt, Belgium | 2000

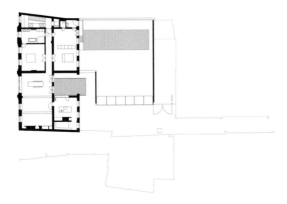

Lino Codato, Antonio Citterio, Edilkamin
Square, Foco, Wall | 2005
Edilkamin

Lizarriturry Tuneu Arquitectura | Girona, Spain
House in Empordà
Empordà, Girona, Spain | 2003

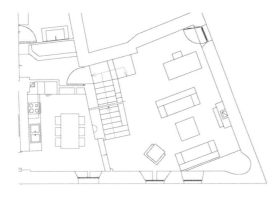

Lundberg Design / Ben Frombgen | San Francisco, CA, USA
Grouf Residence
Healdsburg, CA, USA | 2004

Marc Corbiau | Brussels, Belgium
Contemporary House
Uccle, Brussels, Belgium | 2003

Mauro Munhoz Arquitetura | São Paulo, Brazil
House Bandeira de Mello
Itu, Brazil | 2003

Moriyoshi Naotake Atelier Architects, Takahiro Taji | Tokyo, Japan
Villa in Kitakaurizawa
Kitakaurizawa, Japan | 2004

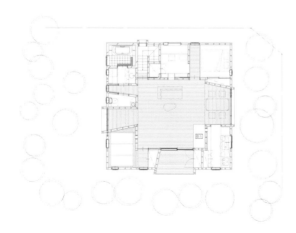

NAT Architecten | Amsterdam, Netherlands
Loft in Eindhoven
Eindhoven, Netherlands | 2005

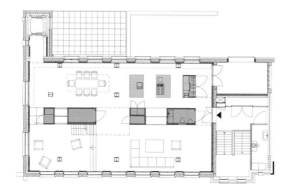

Pich i Aguilera | Barcelona, Spain
House in Tamarit
Tamarit, Tarragona, Spain | 2003

Raymond Morel, Christine Derory | Villefranche-sur-Saône, France
Murano Urban Resort
Paris, France | 2005

Saraiva & Associados/Miguel Saraiva | Lisbon, Portugal
House in Régua
Peso da Régua, Portugal | 2002

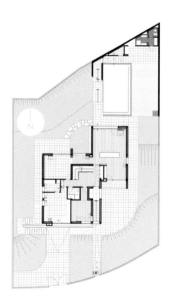

Scheiwiller Svensson Arkitektkontor / Simon Scheiwiller | Stockholm, Sweden
Hotellet
Stockholm, Sweden | 2003

Studio Thun / Matteo Thun | Milan, Italy
Hotel Vigilius
Lana, Italy | 2003

Valdés Arquitectes / Ángel Valdés | Barcelona, Spain
House in Palafolls
Palafolls, Barcelona | 2005

Vladimir Djurovic Landscape Architecture | Broumana, Libanon
Private Residence
Yaafur, Libanon | 2004

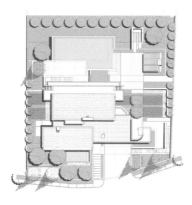

Wolf Udo Wagner
Geniol | 2005
Heinz

Works Architecture / Stephen Quinn, Elise Ovanessoff | London, UK
Flat in Marylebone
London, UK | 2001

Xavier Vendrell, Claudi Agulló | Barcelona, Spain
Casa Abelló
Tamarit, Tarragona, Spain | 2004

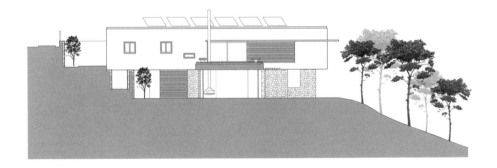

Álvaro Leite Siza Vieira Architect
Rua do Aleixo 53 CV A
4150-043 Porto, Portugal
alvarinhosiza@sapo.pt
Casa Tóló
© Fernando Guerra/FG+SG

Amorphe Takeyama & Associates/Kiyoshi Sey Takeyama
P +81 07 5256 9600
F +81 07 5256 9511
www.amorphe.jp
Kassai House
© Nacása & Partners

Carlos Castanheira & Clara Bastai Arquitectos, Lda.
Rua Conselheiro Veloso da Cruz 61
4400-094 Vila Nova de Gaia, Portugal
P +351 223 704 910
F +351 223 704 908
castanheira.arqtos@net.novis.pt
Casa C. Cast.
© Fernando Guerra/FG+SG

CASA Akira Sakamoto Architect & Associates
1-14-5 Minami-Horie, Nishi-ku, Osaka
Japan Zip 550-0015
P +81 06 6537 1145
F +81 06 6537 1146
casa@akirasakamoto.com
www.akirasakamoto.com
House in Habikigaoka
© Nacása and Partners

Claesson Koivisto Rune Arkitektkontor AB
Sankt Paulsgatan 25
118 48 Stockholm, Sweden
P +46 8 644 58 63
F +46 8 644 58 83
arkitektkontor@claesson-koivisto-rune.se
www.claesson-koivisto-rune.se
House Nº 5
© Ake E:son Lindman

Co.Twee/Christian Van Suetendael & Gert van den Steen
Cuylitsstraat 14
2018 Antwerpen, Belgium
P +32 3 289 43 49
F +32 3 237 68 79
M +32 0475 44 01 79
co@pandora.be
Flat in Schelde
House in Knokke
© Giorgio Possenti/Vega MG

Costa Group
Via Valgraveglia ZAI
19020 Riccò del Golfo
La Spezia, Italy
P +39 01 87 76 93 09
F +39 01 87 76 93 08
info@costagroup.net
www.costagroup.net
Hotel Sant Roc
© Hotel Sant Roc

D'Arcy Jones Design Inc
204-175 Broadway East
BC V5T 1W2, Vancouver, Canada
P +1 604 669 2235
F +1 604 669 2231
mail@darcyjones.com
www.darcyjones.com
Mosewich House
© Undine Pröhl

Delices Architectes/Jean Leclercq
Av. Paul Deschanel 81
1030 Brussels, Belgium
P +32 2 216 36 19
F +32 2 216 06 77
info@delicesarchitectes.com
www.delicesarchitectes.com
Loft Louise
© Laurent Brandajs

Dominique Imbert
Focus
Atelier Dominique Imbert s.a.s.
34380 Viols le Fort, France
P +33 4 67 55 01 93
F +33 4 67 55 77 77
www.focus-creation.com
Cromifocus
Neofocus a bois
Renzofocus
Miofocus
© Focus

EcoSmart Head Office
The Fire Company
10/14 Polo Avenue
Mona Vale NSW 2103, Australia
P +61 2 9997 3050
F +61 2 9997 6050
info@ecosmartfire.com
www.ecosmartfire.com
Oxygen
© The Fire Company

EDENA/Borgers Dumoulin
23 Rue des Glands
1190 Brussels, Belgium
P +32 2 346 20 08/477 35 48 71
F +32 2 343 14 80
edena@skynet.be
Interior design: Anne Derasse
Loft Wery XL
© Laurent Brandajs

EdilKamin SpA
Via Mascagni 7
20020 Lainate, Milan, Italy
P +39 02 93 76 21
F +39 02 93 76 24 00
www.edilkamin.com
Square
Foco
Wall
© Edilkamin

Jordi Galí Estudio

Passatge Forasté 4, entresòl D

08022 Barcelona, Spain

P +34 932 115 442

F +34 932 122 673

jg@jgaliestudi.com

Apartment JG

© Jordi Miralles

Ken Yokogawa Architect & Associates Inc

The Terrace, 1-33-1 Nakamachidai

Tsuzuki-ku, Yokohama

224-0041 Japan

P +81 04 5949 4900

F +81 04 5949 4944

kya@ceres.dti.ne.jp

www.kenyokogawa.co.jp

House in Tateshima

© Nacása & Partners

Laura Cavalca

Via delle Battaglie 40

25122 Brescia, Italy

M +39 335 6921493

lc.studio@libero.it

House in Brescia

© Paolo Basso / Vega MG

Lens Ass Architectuurbureau

Dr. Willemsstraat 19

3500 Hasselt, Belgium

P +32 1 124 77 60

F +32 1 126 21 37

www.lensass.be

Donum

Loft in Hasselt

© Giorgio Possenti / Vega MG

Lizarriturry Tuneu Arquitectura

Castell 6

17256 Palau Sator, Girona, Spain

P +34 972 634 119

lita@coac.net

http://arquitectes.coac.net/ltarquitectura

House in Empordà

© José Luis Hausmann

Lundberg Design / Ben Frombgen

2620 Third Street

94107 San Francisco, CA, USA

P +1 415 695 0110

F +1 415 695 0379

info@lundbergdesign.com

www.lundbergdesign.com

Grouf Residence

© Adrian Gregorutti

Marc Corbiau Architect
78 Avenue de l'Observatoire
1180 Brussels, Belgium
P +32 2 374 20 94
F +32 2 374 97 55
architecture.corbian@skynet.be
Contemporary House
© Laurent Brandajs

Mauro Munhoz Arquitetura
Av. Brigadeiro Luiz Antõnio, 4919 Jardim Paulista
CEP 01401-002 São Paulo, Brasil
P +55 11 3885 9354
F +55 11 3052 3858
mauro@mauromunhoz.arq.br
House Bandeira de Mello
© Nelson Kon

Moriyoshi Naotake Atelier Architects
10th Floor, Toa Build. 1-3-3 Ginza Chuo-Ku
Tokyo, 104-0061, Japan
P +81 03 3567 6511
F +81 03 3567 6515
moriyoshi@j06.itscom.net
Takahiro Taji / Meiji Unv. Taji Lab.
1-1-1, Higasimita, Tama-ku, Kawasaki-city
Kanagawa, 214-8571 Japan
P/F +81 04 4934 7357
taji@isc.meiji.ac.jp
Villa in Kitakaruizawa
© Nacása & Partners

NAT Architecten
Frans Halsstraat 26b
1072 BR Amsterdam, Netherlands
P +31 020 679 0750
F +31 020 675 6444
info@natarchitecten.nl
www.natarchitecten.nl
Loft in Eindhoven
© Peter Cuypers

Pich i Aguilera
Àvila 138, 4.º 1.ª
08018 Barcelona, Spain
P +34 933 016 457
F +34 934 125 223
info@picharchitects.com
www.picharchitects.com
House in Tamarit
© Jordi Miralles

Raymond Morel, Christine Derory
70 Rue Ampere
69400 Villefranche-sur-Saône, France
P +33 4 74 07 20 60
F +33 4 74 07 11 12
groupe-lrd@groupe-lrd.fr
www.muranoresort.com
Murano Urban Resort
© Grégoire Gardette / Murano Urban Resort

Saraiva & Associados Arquitectura e Urbanismo
Rua da Mestra 18-22 Carnide
1600-508 Lisbon, Portugal
P +351 217 120 510
F +351 217 120 511
www.saraivaeassociados.com
House in Régua
© Fernando Guerra/FG+SG

Scheiwiller Svensson Arkitektkontor
Åsögatan 119, 11624 Stockholm, Sweden
P +46 08 5060 1650
F +46 08 5060 1670
www.ssark.se
Hotellet
© James Silverman

Studio Thun/Matteo Thun
Via Appiani 9, 20121 Milan, Italy
P +39 02 65 56 91
F +39 02 65 70 646
info@matteothun.com
www.matteothun.com
Hotel Vigilius
© Agi Simôes/Zapaimages

Valdés Arquitectes/Ángel Valdés
Av. Icària, 164 1.º, 08005 Barcelona, Spain
P +34 932 213 088
F +34 932 213 089
www.valdesarquitectes.com
House in Palafolls
© José Luis Hausmann

Vladimir Djurovic Landscape Architecture
Rizk Plaza, 1st floor, Broumana, Lebanon
www.vladimirdjurovic.com
Private Residence
© Geraldine Bruneel/Vladimir Djurovic Landscape Arch.

Wolf Udo Wagner
Hanauer Landstrasse 161-173
60314 Frankfurt am Main, Germany
P/F +49 69 92 87 05 74
www.wolf-udo-wagner.com
Heinze GmbH & Co Produktions und Vertriebs KG
Ahrstrasse 4, 42117 Wuppertal, Germany
P +49 0202 24257 0
Geniol
© Heinze

Works Architecture/Stephen Quinn, Elise Ovanessoff
16 Upper Montagu Street, W1H 2AN London, UK
P +44 20 7224 8750
F +44 20 7224 8771
studio@worksarchitecture.com
Flat in Marylebone
© Jordi Miralles

Xavier Vendrell, Claudi Agulló
Bailén 28, 2.º 1.ª
08010 Barcelona, Spain
P +34 932 655 486
F +34 932 466 829
vendrell@uic.edu
Casa Abelló
© Jordi Miralles

© 2006 daab
cologne london new york

published and distributed worldwide by
daab gmbh
friesenstr. 50
d - 50670 köln

p + 49-221-94 10 740
f + 49-221-94 10 741

mail@daab-online.com
www.daab-online.com

publisher ralf daab
rdaab@daab-online.com

creative director feyyaz
mail@feyyaz.com

editorial project by loft publications
© 2006 loft publications

editor cristina paredes benítez
layout jonathan roura
english translation jay noden
french translation michel ficerai / lingo sense
italian translation maurizio siliato
german translation susanne engler
copy editing alicia capel tatjer

printed in spain

isbn 3-937718-74-5
dl   B-28621-2006